CONTENTS

INTRODUCTION

By the world's leading pantologist from the University of Lorndret: Sir Horatio Snaptwang

Hello dear reader – and are you sitting comfortably? Of course you are because you're sitting in a nice modern pair of lovely comfortable pants. (Or if you're not wearing pants, you might be sitting in the bath. Or of course you could be sitting in your pants in the bath. Or you could even be sitting in the bath in your pants if your pants are big enough to fit a bath inside.) These days we take pants for granted, but it's incredible to think what an important contribution pants have made to history. When generals lead armies into battle, when great politicians make monumental decisions, when scientists discover new worlds beyond our own, when princes become kings, what do nearly all of them have in common?

Yes, almost all the people who have made their mark in history wore pants, and it's by studying their pants that their marks can be traced. That's why I have devoted my life to collecting pants of all ages, shapes and sizes and putting them into my Museum of Pantology. If you care to delve inside, you'll be amazed at how soon you become familiar with the biggest, hottest, strongest and most uncomfortable pants in history. Indeed, even the smelliest pants in history will be within your grasp. By the time you leave, you will be a fully qualified Pantologist.

So join with me now as I proudly reveal my pants to you in all their glory and introduce you to the fascinating world of pantology!

Pantology ... where every pair tells a story.

And who knows? One day your pants may be able to tell a story of their own...

WARNING: *these days pants are generally regarded as nice, warm, friendly items of comfort, but some of the historic pants in the museum were used as brutal instruments of punishment or pain. Exhibits marked with a* 💀 *should therefore be avoided by readers of a nervous disposition.*

PREHISTORIC PANTS

Could these ancient stone pants be as old as history itself?

The first evidence of man wearing pants comes from the etchings of the great Dutch Pantologist Onn deWere. Previously the metamorphosis of ape into man had been broken into five stages as follows:

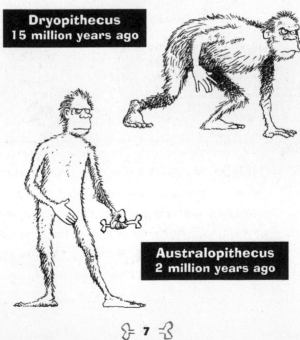

Dryopithecus
15 million years ago

Australopithecus
2 million years ago

Homo habilis
1·5 million years ago

Homo erectus
1 million years ago

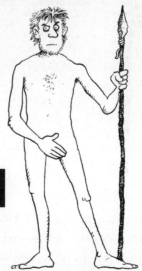

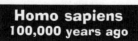

Homo sapiens
100,000 years ago

You'll see that it took 14,900,000 years for man to learn to stand upright, shed most of his body hair and carry his spear, but that left him with an urgent problem. One of his hands was permanently occupied in keeping himself modest, which was especially important if Pantologists were going to do drawings of him. It wasn't until Onn cleverly added the sixth stage that the full story of man's evolutionary success became clear...

Homo pantiens
99,999 years ago

Thanks to his pants, Homo pantiens could now hold spears in both hands and thus he could fully assert his mastery over all the other creatures on the planet.

At the time the first stone pants must have seemed miraculous. Not only did they provide cover, but they also protected the wearer in case he accidentally sat on a cactus plant. But it can't have been long before a few slight disadvantages became obvious. The stone pants were extremely heavy, uncomfortable, draughty, and if they fell down while running they would smash the wearer's toes to bits. Therefore it became essential for Homo pantiens to discover how to make pants from new materials. Here are some examples of pants as they evolved through the ages.

STONE AGE

BRONZE AGE

IRON AGE

WOOLLEN AGE

NYLON AGE

LYCRA AGE

IN TERMS OF EVOLUTION, I THINK THESE WERE A STEP BACKWARDS!

The Pantasaurus

Although man first wore pants 99,999 years ago, there is evidence to suggest that the very first pants appeared on Earth long before that.

The Earth was formed about 4,600 million years ago, and for the first 1,000 million years, vast oceans of boiling chemicals sloshed around and got hit by lightning, blasted by volcanoes and fried by radiation from the sun. Some of these chemicals started reacting to make more complicated compounds and eventually some very simple living cells were formed. For almost the next 3,000 million years, these cells gradually evolved into plant or animal life forms, but one type of cell – known as the polycott – took a strangely different evolutionary course.

According to palaeontologists (people who study fossils), it was on a Tuesday morning about 215 million years ago that the dinosaurs first appeared, and over the next 150 million years lots of different types came and went. These included giants like Diplodocus (27 metres long), the armour-plated Stegosaurus and the Ankylosaurus, that had a heavy-boned tail which it used as a club. As well as land-walking dinosaurs, there were also the flying Pterosaurs and the swimming Plesiosaurs. But although these dinosaurs were very different, they had all evolved following the same simple rule – each creature only had one head and four arms or legs. But the polycott cell was very different.

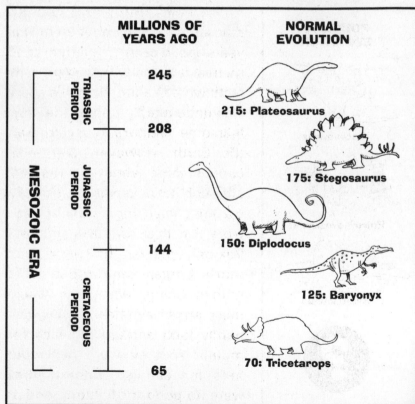

MILLIONS OF
YEARS AGO

NORMAL
EVOLUTION

MESOZOIC ERA

TRIASSIC PERIOD

JURASSIC PERIOD

CRETACEOUS PERIOD

245

208

144

65

215: Plateosaurus

175: Stegosaurus

150: Diplodocus

125: Baryonyx

70: Tricetarops

Although Palaeo-pantologists had managed to trace almost all the completely unpredictable creatures that evolved from the strange polycott cell, it was only recently that they uncovered evidence of the final mutation. This breakthrough came after researchers solved a mystery involving a completely separate creature, the mighty Tyrannosaurus Rex.

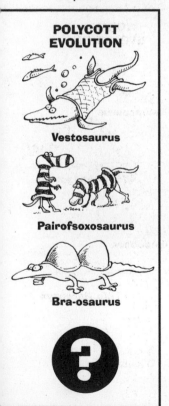

POLYCOTT EVOLUTION

Vestosaurus

Pairofsoxosaurus

Bra-osaurus

?

The T Rex was one of the last dinosaurs. It lived about 70 million years ago, it grew to a length of 15 metres, it stood 6 metres high, its teeth were like bread knives and it was undoubtedly one of the most fearsome creatures ever to walk the Earth. However, the most curious thing about it was that although its head was the size of a washing machine, and its legs were like thick tree trunks, the T Rex only had very tiny arms – not much bigger than those of a human being. What use would these arms have been? They were hardly long enough to reach the mouth, so they were not much help for eating. Certainly they were no good for fighting, and as the T Rex weighed up to 7 tonnes, if it fell over, they would be far too feeble to help it back up again. So what vital purpose could these little arms have?

The academic world had been stuck on this problem for years when the paleo-pantologists found the answer. The breakthrough came while they were studying a tiny scrap of unusual animal hide encrusted into the fossilized hip bone of a T Rex.

PANTASAURUS
SIZE 2 METRES
WASH 40°
50/50 POLYESTER/COTTON

A computer analysis of the DNA configuration revealed that this was a fragment from a previously unknown dinosaur, which has since become known as...

The Pantasaurus

The Pantasaurus grew to a length of around 4 metres from nose to nose and to date it is the only known double-headed dinosaur, the final link in the polycott chain. As each head had independent control of two legs, often it would set off in opposing directions, and over the course of time the skin developed an extraordinary elasticity, in that it could stretch and then resume its original shape again.

Hunting the Pantasaurus would have been difficult as both heads would be on the lookout for predators. However, if a wary T Rex managed to approach from the side, the Pantasaurus could be killed by knocking it on to its back and taking a deep bite from the midriff. The inner flesh, legs and bones, along with both heads and necks, would then be consumed by the T Rex, leaving just the hide which would resemble the pant shape with which we all are familiar today.

When the dinosaurs first appeared, the Earth was quite hot, but over the next 145 million years it cooled down. By the time the T Rex arrived it would have been distinctly chilly, so despite having a tiny brain, the T Rex devised a cunning use for the Pantasaurus hide to keep itself warm and cosy. It would insert its legs into the gap where it had bitten into the midriff, and push its feet out through the neck holes. The only remaining problem was how to pull the pants up, and experts are now convinced that T Rex's distinctly small arms evolved purely to enable this operation. The arms were perfectly positioned to reach down, pull the pants up and then hold them in place, thus allowing the T Rex to continue in its activities feeling safe and secure.

It is well documented that the dinosaurs died out around 65 million years ago, probably due to a large meteor hitting the Earth. What is not known is whether the mothers of all the T Rex's had insisted they put on clean Pantasauruses that morning – but rest assured, valuable research into this mystery still continues.

The Genesis of Pants

A set of old wall paintings recently discovered in the ancient French chapel at Frey de la Stique has added an exciting new dimension to one of the world's oldest stories. Pantologists are now suggesting that the start of the Bible should read as follows:

In the beginning there was the garden of Eden. This contained a man, a big selection of trees and lots of animals, but most importantly it did not contain any pants. God called the man Adam and told him that he could go round giving all the animals names. What's more, Adam was allowed to eat any fruit he liked from the trees – all apart from one apple tree, the Tree of the Knowledge of Good and Evil. God told Adam that the fruit on the tree was forbidden and if he ate any of those apples he'd die. In fact, even if he just touched the apples he'd die, so Adam left them well alone.

After a while Adam got rather bored, so God decided to give him someone to talk to. When Adam was asleep, God took one of his ribs and made it into a woman called Eve. When Adam woke up he was rather surprised that one little rib had been made into a someone as big as he was. He was even more surprised to find that she was his wife and he was her husband because he didn't actually remember the wedding. However this would not be the last time a man woke up to find he'd got married without knowing it (indeed, it still happens today). So Adam had a wife and Eve had a husband – but so far neither of them had any pants. This didn't seem to bother them and they toddled round quite happily eating fruit until one day they bumped into a talking serpent. Naturally the conversation soon turned to the subject of eating fruit because that's all they ever did. Eve happened to mention that they could eat any fruit they liked except the apples from the Tree of the Knowledge of Good and Evil because if they ate them or even just touched them, then they would die.

No you won't actually.

Try them. Go on, I dare you.

So Eve very carefully prodded one of the forbidden apples with her finger and found she did not die. She then pulled the apple off the branch and ate it, and liked it so much that she got Adam to eat an apple too. They were chomping their way through piles of the forbidden fruit when they suddenly looked up and caught sight of each other.

…they both cried out in astonishment, because the apples from the tree had given them the knowledge of what being naked was about. It was at that moment that they realized God had been telling the truth about the apples killing them, because they both nearly died of embarrassment.

"Eeek!" the two did yelleth out in shame – but all was not lost. Luckily for them the knowledge from the tree had not only included good and evil, but also a section on how to improvise underwear, so off they ran to make themselves some pants out of fig leaves.

When God saw Adam was hiding behind a bush trying to make some pants from inconveniently shaped leaves, he asked what was going on. Adam admitted to eating the forbidden apples, but said it was all Eve's idea. God then asked Eve why she'd done it, and she said it was the serpent's idea. God then got into a mighty rage and summoned the serpent before him.

"Oh serpent," spaketh God crossly, "I had finished making all the other animals in the garden, but I hadn't finished making you. I still had some legs I was going to stick on, BUT as a punishment for interfering, you can't have them now."

And thus the serpent would suffer for ever in two different ways. First, he would always spend his life crawling around on his belly rather than being able to walk. And second, the serpent would never experience the warm comforting feeling that can 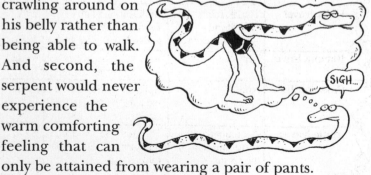 only be attained from wearing a pair of pants.

Bearing in mind the limited range of underwear material available to Adam and Eve they made a wise choice – as the following table shows:

	GOOD POINTS	BAD POINTS	SCORE
Fig leaves	Quite large	Big gaps in the leaf; fall down in autumn	6/10
Holly leaves	Tough, nice colour and shiny appearance	Spiky; too small; berries might be pecked off by birds	2/10
Banana leaves	Very big	May attract monkeys looking for bananas	9/10
Pine needles	None	Spiky; tiny; fall all over the floor at Christmas	0/10
Apple leaves	Accompanied by pretty blossom in the spring	Fall down in autumn; attract bees and wasps; quite small	3/10

HOW FAMOUS PEOPLE DRIED THEIR PANTS

NO.1 ADAM AND EVE

ANCIENT PANTS
The Trojan Pants

These pants are a reconstruction of the very first pair of pants ever used in armed conflict. They date from around 3,300 years ago, when there was a bit of a mix-up in ancient Greece.

The most beautiful woman in the world at the time was called Helen. She had fallen in love with a prince named Paris, who had taken her to his home town of Troy. Unfortunately, Helen was married to King Menelaus of Sparta who was a bit miffed that his wife had done a runner and sent his brother Agamemnon to get her back. Agamemnon took 1,000 ships full of soldiers over to Troy, but not surprisingly Paris's father, King Priam didn't let them in.

This Greek urn tells the full story!

After the Greek soldiers had sat outside Troy for ten years, they realized that they ought to start working out a plan B – something different, devious and desperate. Little was known of this plan until modern pantologists happened across some fragments of an ancient Greek urn. By studying the pictures on these fragments, we managed to piece together the finer details of this extraordinary story.

Plan B was this: as the Trojans were refusing to surrender, the Greeks would pretend to surrender instead. Naturally the Trojans didn't trust them. Why should the Greeks suddenly surrender? Why didn't they just sail home and leave them alone? It was then that Agamemnon said: "All I ask, on behalf of my brother Menelaus, is to plant one kiss on the beautiful Helen of Troy."

This seemed like a reasonable request, but the Trojans were still wary. They had no intention of letting Helen out of the city while the Greeks were still around, so they would have to let Agamemnon in. But how could they be sure he was unarmed? It was Agamemnon himself who made the suggestion: "I will approach wearing nothing but a pair of pants."

It seemed safe enough to the Trojans and they agreed. Unknown to them however, the night before Agamemnon was due to approach the city gates, there was much activity in the Greek encampment. Needles flashed in the torchlight as lashings of cloth were meticulously stitched together to create a

pair of pants the like of which had never been seen before. Within this pair of normal-looking pants were three secret cavities, each large enough to conceal a fully armed soldier. The plan was simple: once he was safely within the walls of Troy, Agamemnon would lower his pants to release the soldiers, who would then make for the gatehouse, overpower the guards and open up the city to the invaders. It was foolproof.

Agamemnon next had to decide who should be smuggled into Troy. Every member of the Greek force had volunteered so lots were drawn and the honour of hiding in his pants fell to Buttrappus, Shredes and Dimpuldas.

As dawn broke, the volunteers took their places in the folds of material and then, with the help of several burly attendants, Agamemnon pulled on the great pants. The waistband came nearly to his neck, and while three of the attendants held it in place, a fourth fastened the pants tight with a large belt to ensure they did not fall prematurely. Out of view of the city, Agamemnon practised taking a few steps to get used to the extra weight, while inside the pants the volunteers tried to stop their swords and daggers from sticking through the material and jabbing into him as they were being tumbled and jostled around.

A trumpet sounded high on the battlements of Troy, then a small gate opened, just wide enough to allow one person wearing nothing more than a pair of massive pants to step inside. Very cautiously Agamemnon walked to the gateway and then squeezed through. The gate was immediately closed and bolted behind him. To either side of him stood lines of armed soldiers, but his gaze was immediately drawn to the gap directly in front of him.

There, across the city square, was a marble throne on which sat the most beautiful woman he had ever seen. She was dressed in a shimmering silk robe of purple and gold, and the sunlight glinted off the jewels set  in her hair. There could be no doubt who she was.

This was the lady whose face had launched 1,000 ships – the legendarily beautiful Helen of Troy.

"Psst!" came a voice from his gusset. "Is it time to get out yet?"

"No!" Agamemnon whispered back. "There's too many people watching! I'll tell you when."

Slowly, and with great dignity, Agamemnon walked across the city square towards the figure on the marble throne. With every step he took towards her she seemed more beautiful to him. Agamemnon could not tear his eyes away – he had long wondered if she was really worth all the inconvenience of ten years' camping outside a locked city. From the first instance he saw her, he knew the answer. She was.

Agamemnon was so captivated by Helen's beauty, that he didn't notice Paris and his father King Priam looking down from a nearby balcony. Beside them was the King's daughter Cassandra, who had led an interesting life. The god Apollo had been so smitten by her that he had given her the gift of prophecy, but when she made it clear that she wasn't so keen on him, the god arranged it so that nobody would ever believe her.

"Look, father!" cried Cassandra as Agamemnon waddled across the city square. "Don't you think there's something suspicious about him?"

"She could be right father," said Paris. "Those are very big pants."

"Rubbish," said the King. "I've seen bigger."

"Doom impends!" wailed Cassandra, clutching her hand to her forehead. "There's something hiding in those massive pants that could destroy our whole city."

"Don't be silly," said the King, giving her a bored look. He was used to his daughter being melodramatic.

"Why doesn't anyone ever believe me?" moaned Cassandra. "It's true, I tell you, doom impends."

"No it isn't true, but if it makes you feel better..." The King turned back to face the city square and shouted: "STOP!"

As the echoes of the King's command died away, Agamemnon reluctantly halted, his eyes still fixed on Helen of Troy.

"Your pants – they seem very big," cried the King. "What size are they?"

Agamemnon suddenly came to his senses and realized where he was and the potential danger he was in. Fortunately he had been prepared for this question and had an answer ready.

"Fourteen and a half," admitted Agamemnon. "To be honest I've been trying to get down to a twelve, but what with sitting outside your city for ten years, I just haven't been getting the exercise."

King Priam exchanged a glance with Paris and they both nodded. It seemed a reasonable reply.

"Fair enough," called out King Priam. "You may proceed."

"No!" wailed Cassandra, but she was ignored.

Finally Agamemnon reached the beautiful Helen.

"Good sir," she smiled at him. Her voice was as soft and sweet as the chime of a crystal bell being flicked by a butterfly's wing. "Pray, which cheek would you kiss – the left or the right?"

Agamemnon almost blushed. Both her cheeks were so very beautiful, he could not decide. Sensing his embarrassment she smiled.

"Or perhaps you would care to kiss between the two?"

And with that she leaned forwards, her lips ready to exchange a kiss. Agamemnon closed his eyes in rapture, but just before contact was made...

"Shall we get out now?" came a voice from his pants.

"Shhh!" hissed Agamemnon.

"Did you hear a voice?" asked Helen, drawing back.

"No!" said Agamemnon. "I did not!"

"Then you shall have your kiss," she said. Again she leaned forwards and again Agamemnon prepared himself for the joy of her caress.

"So when are we coming out then?" said another voice from the pants.

"Shuttup!" snapped Agamemnon.

"The sound comes from your pants!" gasped Helen. "I heard them speak!"

"That's impossible," exclaimed Agamemnon. He looked down and deliberately directed his voice towards the great pants. "My pants did not speak, but if they do speak then they are DEAD."

"What's going on?" King Priam whispered to Paris.

"I don't know," said Paris. "He seems to be talking to his pants."

"I told you!" wailed Cassandra. "There's something evil in there that will destroy us all."

They watched as once again Helen of Troy leaned forwards towards Agamemnon, her lips ready. And once again the warrior King closed his eyes and leaned towards her.

"Oh come on, let us out!" said a voice from the pants.

"We've been in here for ages," declared another.

"Yeah, some of us are getting pretty hot down here," replied a third.

"It was your pants!" said Helen, pulling back. "I definitely heard them. Will they speak again?"

Agamemnon shook his head, then clenched his eyes tight shut and gritted his teeth in concentration. Suddenly a very different noise came from the rear of the great pants.

"Ahhh! That was a sound of my own making," smiled Agamemnon triumphantly. "And now I can promise that the pants will not speak again."

And indeed, from within the pants came the sounds of coughing and gasping and then all fell deadly quiet. Helen of Troy's nose wrinkled and her eyes started to water.

"Well?" Agamemnon asked, puckering his lips. "How about it then?"

"Sorry," she replied trying not to breathe too deeply. "For some reason I'm no longer in the mood."

Agamemnon's shoulders fell and he took a step backwards.

"Another time then?" he asked hopefully.

"Sure," said Helen clasping a handkerchief across her face. "I'll get my people to talk to your people, we'll fix something up."

Slowly Agamemnon turned and headed back to leave through the little gateway. Up on the balcony Paris nudged Cassandra.

"You got it wrong as usual, sister," he sniggered. "There's not much in those pants that will damage us now."

That night in the Greek camp, the whole army was in despair. Their best plan had failed, so they decided to abandon Troy and go home. They had already started packing up their ships, when a young guard approached Agamemnon and made a suggestion:

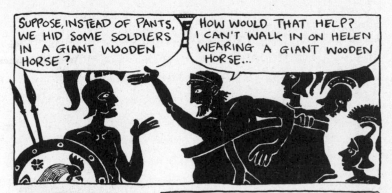

SUPPOSE, INSTEAD OF PANTS, WE HID SOME SOLDIERS IN A GIANT WOODEN HORSE?

HOW WOULD THAT HELP? I CAN'T WALK IN ON HELEN WEARING A GIANT WOODEN HORSE...

NO SIRE, WE PRETEND WE'RE SETTING OFF HOME, BUT WE JUST HIDE AND LEAVE THE HORSE BEHIND. WHEN THE TROJANS SEE IT THEY'LL DRAG IT INTO THE CITY. WHEN THEY'RE ALL ASLEEP, OUR MEN WILL JUMP OUT, UNLOCK THE GATES, AND WE ALL CHARGE IN AND MASSACRE THEM.

I DON'T KNOW ABOUT THAT. IT SOUNDS A BIT FAR-FETCHED.

ADMITTEDLY IT'S NOT AS GOOD AS YOUR PANTS PLAN.

OF COURSE IT'S NOT. THAT'S WHY YOU'RE ONLY A GUARD WHOSE NAME NOBODY WILL REMEMBER AND I'M A GREAT KING.

OH ALL RIGHT THEN. WE'LL GIVE IT A GO. WHAT HAVE WE GOT TO LOSE?

As so often happens in history, it is the sensible plans that fail and the unlikely plans that succeed. And even though Cassandra warned against bringing the horse into the city, she was ignored and thus Troy was destroyed and its people either slaughtered or enslaved. And thus it is that the tale of the Trojan Horse has been repeated for 33 centuries ... and if it hadn't been for the discovery of the mosaic pants, the tale of the Trojan Pants would now be completely forgotten.

Egyptian Pants

ANCIENT EGYPTIAN PANTS HAD THE LEG-HOLES AT THE FRONT AND BACK RATHER THAN THE SIDES...

THUS ENABLING THE WEARER TO WALK IN THE CORRECT EGYPTIAN MANNER...

The ancient Egyptians took their pants very seriously as we can see by these tomb paintings from the year 48 BC. They depict the first meeting between the Roman emperor Julius Caesar and the Egyptian queen whom he was destined to fall in love with.

This is just one of the many myths and legends concerning the pants of Ancient Egypt, but the strangest story of them all begins over 1,200 years earlier and it involves the most valuable exhibit in our museum.

THE CURSED PANTS OF QUEEN PARPUNSNIFFET
A Poor Burial

In 1290 BC, the greatest pharaoh who ever ruled Egypt came to power. Ramses II lived to be 96 years old, and as well as keeping charge of the Upper and Lower Nile regions, he created some of the finest buildings the world has ever seen, including the two magnificent temples carved into the cliffs of Abu Simbel and the great Hypostyle hall at Karnak. The great Ramses is also famous for having about 200 wives. His first and favourite wife was probably Nefertari, but among the many that have been overlooked or forgotten was one Nubian beauty called Parpunsniffet.

Sadly, Parpunsniffet died on the night of her wedding, and as Ramses already had three other weddings planned that week, arrangements for her burial were made rather hastily. Usually an Egyptian queen would be buried in a deep tomb guarded by statues of gods, and this would be at the end of a long secret underground passageway, sealed off with enormous blocks of granite. But as Parpunsniffet had only been queen for a few hours, the burial party felt that she wasn't really worth the effort, so they just plonked her in a coffin and wandered around trying to decide how to dispose of her.

By chance, the waters of the Nile were particularly low that night, and they noticed a small hole low in the riverbank. It turned out to be the opening to a short tunnel, which led to a cavity just about large enough to serve as a tomb. Soon Queen Parpunsniffet's wooden coffin had been dumped inside along with a few statues of Egyptian deities to keep her company. As she had hardly earned the title of Queen, she didn't get any of the good deities such as Ra (the sun god, with a hawk's head) or Hathor (the goddess of love, with a cow's head). Instead she got some long-forgotten C-list deities including Sharab (the god of impromptu wind, with the crocodile head), Khnoram (the god of embarrassment, with a snake head), Dhup (the goddess of sudden loud noises, with the duck head).

Just as the waters were rising again and the burial party was leaving the riverbank the high priest Abassama realized something terrible: Parpunsniffet was still wearing her bridal outfit –

and that included her fabulous diamond-encrusted golden wedding pants. These pants were a treasure for which many would risk their lives, and yet they had left her in a tomb that was barely hidden and not properly sealed. Already the river water was pouring into the tunnel. There was only one thing that the anxious priest could do. Raising his face to the full moon and spreading his arms wide, he laid a curse of the dead on the pants of Parpunsniffet. Anyone trying to steal the pants would fall foul of the three deities that guarded her.

And so the young queen was laid to rest, watched over by her little gods, but she was not to be untroubled for ever...

An Ill Wind

About 100 years after the death of Queen Parpunsniffet, two grave robbers were sailing down the Nile. The waters were low enough for them to spot the opening in the riverbank, so they crawled inside and discovered the warped and mould-covered coffin. When they ripped the lid away they were so excited to see the golden pants that they failed to notice the eyes of the statues around them flickering into life. The next piece of scroll tells the rest of the story.

Soon the two brothers were back on their boat with the wedding pants safely stowed in a basket at the back. Thanks to the southerly wind and the flow of the river, they were able to make good time sailing up the Nile. One hundred miles away was the port of Alexandria, and it was there that they hoped a foreign trader would give them a good price for the pants without too many questions being asked.

As night fell two days later they found themselves passing the lights of the ancient port. At last it was time to slow down and look for a suitable landing point, so they lowered their sail. However, rather than slowing down, the boat picked up speed. Faster and faster it careered through the water, leaving a white wake behind it. Sailors on other vessels cursed and called out to them to stop, but the brothers had lost control.

"How is it that we are still sailing at such speed?" moaned the elder of the two brothers.

"I know not," replied the younger. "For the sail is put away, so how can the wind be blowing us?"

It was then that they realized they were being blown by a different wind. From the basket at the back of the boat, great and powerful gusts were blasting, thrusting the small vessel forwards. By this time the river had widened out so much that they could no longer see the banks on either side, and the still surface of the water was being broken by black waves, growing ever larger and larger. Soon the lights of Alexandria were behind them and the tranquility of the Nile had given way to the raging Mediterranean Sea.

"The wind blows from the pants!" cried the eldest. "We must throw them overboard or we shall be lost in the great waters."

The two brothers reached for the basket, but were immediately driven back. Their eyes watered and they both held their noses.

"Such a foul wind I never did smell!" cried the eldest, clutching his belly.

"I cannot breathe again of it for fear of losing my guts," said the youngest. "We would be better taking our chances in the sea!"

And so together the two brothers leapt from the boat. Far away on the horizon the distant lights of Alexandria still glimmered in the dark, and they splashed out towards them. But they were not alone in that sea, for behind them a pair of cold eyes stuck out from the surface of the water. The first they were aware of the crocodile was when the eldest brother lost the toes on his left foot. With a scream he warned his brother to swim faster, but it was too late. The younger had already suffered a similar fate. They splashed away in a mad panic, trying to outswim the crocodile, but Sharab took his time. Piece by piece he nipped off their toes, feet, ankles, calves, knees ... and kept on going until just their heads remained, still trying to paddle along with their ears. Then with a final snap of his jaws, they were both gone.

The boat itself continued out across the open sea, bearing the cursed pants of Queen Parpunsniffet...

The Travels of the Pants

There is evidence to suggest that over the next 2,000 years the wedding pants travelled all around the world, and wherever they went they were protected by the curse.

This Arabian rug suggests that one would-be pant thief tried to ride across the desert wearing the golden pants. But the horse threw him, miles from nowhere, and the heat of the sun caused the pants to get so hot that they roasted him to death.

Yet another cursed occurrence is shown in this carved walrus tusk. Clearly the Inuit wearing the pants was up to no good, as the weight of the golden pants has pulled him through the bottom of his kayak.

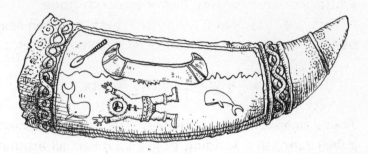

And it was very unwise for this mountaineering pant-snatcher to be wearing the golden pants during a thunderstorm.

HOW QUEEN PARPUNSNIFFET'S PANTS CAME TO THE MUSEUM OF PANTOLOGY

The staff at the museum were most disappointed when they saw the following newspaper article:

We had been studying Egyptian pantology for many years, and not surprisingly we were desperate to get our hands on the queen's golden pants. It was therefore a great disappointment when they were accidentally discovered at the bottom of the sea by Glutten Oil Inc. Harvey Glutten never had any respect for pantology, and rather than treat the pants with the respect they deserved, he wanted to use them to make as much money as possible. He planned to launch the pants in a huge blaze of publicity, and had invited all the top celebrities to be there. Of course, there was nothing we could do about it, but the pants themselves had other ideas.

Harvey had arranged a fabulous garden party full of actors, models, politicians and rock stars. The last guests to arrive were the Prime Minister and his wife, and as soon as they turned up he invited them to join him on a stage in front of an army of television cameras from all around the world.

The Prime Minister's wife had dressed to suit the occasion, and as this occasion was full of film stars, rock musicians and fashion models, she was wearing an outfit comprising mainly chains, ropes and safety pins. She was standing between her husband and Harvey when he made his big announcement.

> Ladies and gentlemen, I'd like to thank the Prime Minister and his lovely wife for joining us at the unveiling of the oldest pants in the world. And now please welcome the lady who will be wearing them this evening ... Miss Tutu Breathless!

There was a polite round of applause as a very elegant lady stepped up on to the stage. Tutu Breathless was the most fabulous supermodel on the planet, and she was wearing a special dress that hung down in two sections from the waistband. To her side dangled a piece of cord; when it was pulled, the sections of the dress would slide apart like curtains, revealing the golden pants she was wearing. By now Harvey was so excited that he could hardly get his next words out.

"Ladies and gentlemen, as I promised, please show your appreciation for the oldest pants in the world."

Harvey reached out, grabbed the cord and pulled.

Now maybe it was an accident, or maybe the cursed pants had something to do with it, but whatever it was, the crowd gasped in shock – and no wonder! The pants they found themselves looking at were not the oldest pants in the world, but judging by appearances, they might have been the second-oldest pants in the world.

In all the excitement, Harvey had reached out the wrong hand, and the cord he had pulled was part of the Prime Wife's dress, which had completely fallen apart. There, for all to see, was the Prime Wife wearing her comfortable old serge blue, heavily patched hiking bloomers, handed down from her granny's Girl Guide days. Within one second the cameras had flashed the Prime Pants right around the world. Within two seconds the Prime Wife's left fist had smashed into Harvey's jaw and within three seconds he was tumbling off the stage. It just so happened that a waiter was walking past with a tray of party snacks; Harvey Glutten fell on them and he was immediately skewered by 100 extra-long cocktail sticks.

Rumour had it that the waiter had a black forked tongue, which leads pantologists to wonder: could this tragedy have been the work of the snake god Khnoram?

Meanwhile, when Tutu Breathless realized that none of the cameras were on her, she hurriedly sneaked off in the opposite direction, and leapt into a taxi for the airport. She hoped to escape with the golden wedding pants, but again some strange force was about to prevent her.

At the airport, Tutu was making her way to the departure lounge, but first she had to join the queue to get past the airport security barrier. There was a little archway that everybody had to walk under, and when the man in front of her stepped through it, an alarm went off.

 BEEP BEEP BEEP

The noise wasn't very loud, but it was enough to make two large security guards step forward. Tutu was a bit worried – she'd forgotten about the metal detector – but then she shrugged her shoulders. So what if the golden pants set the little alarm off? There was no need to worry. The security people were only looking for weapons, and pants weren't a weapon so she'd be all right. She stepped under the arch.

The alarm let rip with such a high-decibel gusset gale that Tutu leapt right out of the golden pants, which clattered to the floor at her feet. When she saw everybody staring at her and giggling, she screamed in embarrassment and ran straight out of the airport.

"Wow!" said one of the guards. "I never heard the alarm go off like that before!"

Everybody in the airport was completely stunned – all, that is, except one. Waiting behind Tutu in the queue had been a small figure in a coat with a turned-up collar, and she was making a soft strange noise, something between a laugh and a quack. Could this have been Dhup, the goddess of unexpected loud noises?

Meanwhile the question remained, what should be done with the abandoned pants? By now people had begun to suspect they were cursed, and in the end the authorities were only too pleased when we offered to house them in our museum. We knew we had to treat the pants with extreme caution, so to make them feel at home we tried to recreate the last resting place of Queen Parpunsniffet. The display was made to look like a hole in a riverbank, and we decorated it with Egyptian writing and pictures. But when we came to put the pants up on display, we found that the strangest thing had happened – three little old statues had somehow appeared in the background. We have no idea where they came from or how they got there, but there's one thing for certain ... now that we've got them safely mounted, we won't be taking the Queen's pants down again.

The Eighth Wonder of the Ancient World

Nearly everybody has heard of the Seven Wonders of the World, but pantologists have discovered new evidence to suggest that there may have been one more...

The Seven Wonders were: the Pyramids of Egypt, the Hanging Gardens of Babylon, the Statue of Zeus, the Temple of Artemis at Ephesus in Greece, the Mausoleum of Halicarnassus, the Pharos of Alexandria (a giant lighthouse) and the Colossus of Rhodes.

To pantologists, the Colossus is the most interesting of the seven – a 30-metre-high bronze statue of Helios, the Greek god of the sun, and it was built to guard the harbour entrance on the island of Rhodes. It took 12 years to build and was completed in 282 BC; 56 years later it was destroyed by an earthquake. The pieces of the Colossus lay there for about 1,000 years until a Syrian bought them, and it took 900 camels to carry these all away.

For more than 2,000 years people have puzzled over one big mystery: how exactly did the Colossus guard the harbour? At last pantologists have discovered the answer, and in doing so they have uncovered what surely must be regarded as the Eighth Wonder of the Ancient World – The Humungous Pants of Helios.

The pantological theory is that if the Colossus was to guard the harbour, it must have been standing astride the narrow entrance so that any ships coming into Rhodes would have to sail between its legs. Friendly ships would be allowed to pass through unhindered, but if any enemy ships were sighted, the entire harbour could be secured very quickly in the most ingenious manner. Helios would simply allow his pants to fall down around his ankles, thus blocking the entrance.

Yes indeed, pantologists are now convinved that the Colossus was wearing the biggest pair of pants the world has ever known. Knowing that the statue was 30 metres high, a team of highly specialized mathepanticians have gone on to prove that the size of the pants was XXXXXXXXXXXXXXL – which works out to be approximately 15 metres around the waistband. Further calculations reveal that these pants would be big enough to go around about 200 normal adult humans without being unduly stretched. What's more, if Helios the sun god ever wanted to tuck his shirt-tail into his pants, the tail would be about the size of 18-bed sheets sewn together.

The Humungous Pants were made from the leather of over 600 oxen and were held in place around the waistband by a selection of iron hooks. These hooks were linked via an ingenious mechanism to the dropping lever – which when pulled would cause the hooks to retract inside the body and so allow the pants to fall. The lower part of the gusset was studded with heavy lead weights so that any ship passing underneath would be crushed against the bottom of the harbour mouth. Once the enemy had retreated, the pants would be hoisted back into place by a strong rope that came out of a hole around the back of the statue, and which was connected to counterweights that ran down inside the statue's legs.

Although some doubt has been cast on these theories by conventional historians, there is one undeniable piece of evidence that confirms the pants' existence. Like any other pants, these required washing. The problem was finding a place where such humungous pants could be put out to dry – and it was for this very purpose that the ancient people constructed another of the ancient wonders of the world: the Hanging Gardens of Babylon.

The Pantajabbus Combat Pants

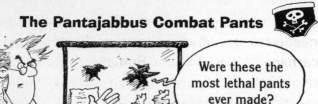

Were these the most lethal pants ever made?

A few scraps of leather, a rusty metal spike and some old pieces of parchment ... these are the only remains we have of one of the most remarkable pairs of pants ever discovered. To understand more, we take you back to the time of the Roman gladiators.

In the year 264 BC one of the old Roman leaders called Junius Brutus died, and in honour of his death, his sons arranged for three pairs of gladiators to kill each other in front of a large crowd. Everybody who was at the funeral enjoyed it so much that the idea immediately caught on, and soon all Rome's wealthiest citizens were hosting enormous fight shows. There was so much blood flying about that the organizers would always ensure that the ground was covered in lots of sand to soak it all up. This sand was called "harena" and that's how the stadiums where these fights were held became known as "arenas".

The gladiators themselves were usually captured enemy soldiers, who were kept in special training camps where they learnt all the lethal skills they needed to stay alive in the arena. To stop the endless carnage getting dull, the Romans had different sorts of gladiators to liven things up. Here are some of the most common ones:

Name	Weapons	Armour	Usual opponent
RETIARIUS ("The Net-man")	Trident, net, dagger	Metal shoulder-plate; thick left sleeve	Secutores or Murmillo
SECUTORES ("The Pursuer")	Sword; rectangular shield	Helmet; protection on right arm and left leg	Retarius
MURMILLO	Sword; curved shield	Helmet with fish-shaped fin; right-arm protection	Almost anyone
THRAEX	Small curved sword; small shield	Hemet with a big brim; metal shinpads	Murmillo

You'll notice that the details of the weapons and armour are very exact. Everything was carefully calculated to make sure nobody had the advantage, otherwise the fights would be over too quickly and it wouldn't be nearly so much fun.

There are also records of many other types of gladiators, including Dimachaeri who used two swords at once, Equites who fought on horseback with a spear and a sword, Essedari who fought on chariots, and Hoplomachi and Samnites who wore full armour and had spears and small shields. When swords and spears got boring there were the Laquerii who used looped ropes, the Andabatae

who had huge helmets without eyeholes so they just charged at each other blindly, and Bestiarii who tried to fight exotic animals such as elephants armed only with a spear or knife. To put people in the mood before the carnage started, there were even clown gladiators called Praegenarii. Music would play and they would run on and hit each other with wooden swords.

Pantologists are now able to add to this illustrious list, thanks to their discovery of a few pages from the work of the Roman poet Baggidrors. His epic *Ode to Undies* indicates that in the year 49 BC in the arena at Frillinnix, several of the toughest and meanest gladiators were lined up ready to face a completely new and untested type of challenger, but when he first stepped out on to the bloodied sands, everyone gasped. He wore no armour – not even a helmet – and did not carry a sword or a shield. The audience yawned and the other gladiators sniggered because they all thought that he would be dead in a few seconds. How wrong they were.

The Pantajabbus simply wore a pair of thick leather pants, but sticking out from them in all directions was a set of long sharp metal spikes. He also wore large boots with springs fixed to the soles, and in his hand he carried a very long sheet of paper wound up into a roll.

As was customary for a new gladiator, the officials invited him to choose which of the other gladiators he'd care to fight first, although they were probably thinking that the first fight of the Pantajabbus would also be his last. Some of the crowd were already getting up to leave – but they hurried back when they saw to their amazement that the Pantajabbus had torn several squares from his roll of paper and had flicked one at each of the other gladiators. The signal was clear – the Pantajabbus was challenging them all at once.

The judge raised his hand for silence and then called out "*Morituri te Salutamus*" the famous cry that means "Those about to die, we salute you". It was time to begin.

The sun beat down and glistened on the sweat-covered muscles of the gladiators. Their swords and daggers were ready, they were just waiting for the Pantajabbus to make the first move. They were unsure whether he would charge towards them or simply run away, but what they hadn't expected was for him to take a huge leap straight up into the air. Down he came and then up he leapt again, this time rising even higher, boosted by the springs on his boots. Again and again he jumped and they could only stand in astonishment as he bounced his way towards them and then leapt right over their heads.

On reaching the far side of the arena he bounced on the spot, ripped more pieces from the roll and flicked them at the noses of the others.

The Murmillo's patience broke first. With a scream he ran towards the Pantajabbus, his sword held high, but the Pantajabbus was ready. Unrolling a long section of paper, he executed a huge bounce and somersaulted right over the Murmillo, wrapping the paper around his face as he did so. The Murmillo staggered around, blindly pulling the paper away, but those moments of hesitation cost him his life. The Pantajabbus made a low, hard bounce backwards, bringing his legs up, and stabbed the Murmillo in the chest with his spiky pants. The crowd loved it. It was the first time they had seen an armed bottom used in combat.

Next came the Retarius, waving his net and trident, but once again the Pantajabbus was ready. Throwing himself feet first against the wall, he shot backwards, smashing his pants on to the net-man's jaw and knocking him to the sand.

The two-sworded Dimachaerus and the Laquerius now both stepped forwards. The Laquerius waved his lasso around his head, but the Pantajabbus was too quick and had already tied a loop in the end of his paper roll. Leaping right over the swinging rope, the Pantajabbus draped his paper around the neck of the Dimachaerus and heaved. Caught off balance, the two swords of the Dimachaerus plunged straight through the Laquerius, and before the swordsman could apologize, the Pantajabbus had landed bottom-first on his head.

The only gladiator left was the huge Andabatae in his heavy eyeless helmet. Even the merciless Pantajabbus was at a loss as to what to do, for there was no honour to be gained in defeating the sightless giant. The Andabatae had no idea that he was the only one of his comrades left standing, and could never have imagined the dreadful weapon he was facing. If the Pantajabbus were to attack and kill the almost-helpless Andabatae, the crowd may well turn against him, and he might face execution himself.

But fortune smiled on the Pantajabbus that day, for with a mighty cry the Andabatae charged off in completely the wrong direction, tripped up on the Retarius's net, slammed his head into a wall and knocked himself out.

Sadly the Pantajabbus was never to appear in combat again. After the success of his first day in the arena, he spent the whole night celebrating so wildly that when he woke up the next morning, he was feeling distinctly groggy. As he was getting out of bed, he made a silly little mistake. It's a mistake that everybody has made at some point or other in their lives, but for the Pantajabbus it proved fatal. He pulled his pants on inside out.

HOW FAMOUS PEOPLE DRIED THEIR PANTS
NO. 2 QUEEN BOUDICA

MEDIEVAL PANTS
The Royal Pant Line

OF COURSE THESE AREN'T THE REAL CROWN JEWELS...

History has seen billions of pairs of common pants come and go, but there is one special pair of pants that has lasted for almost 1,200 years. In this time these pants have had over 60 different owners and have been responsible for many bloody battles and foul murders. These are the Royal Coronation Pants, and although their existence is still a closely guarded secret to the general public, they represent the foundation on which the whole of the British monarchy sits. Naturally these pants are of great interest to pantologists, who have worked long and hard to reveal the traces of history that they may contain.

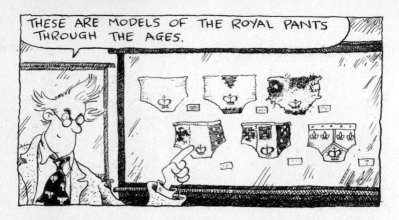

THESE ARE MODELS OF THE ROYAL PANTS THROUGH THE AGES.

THE ORIGINAL ANGLO-SAXON PANTS, AD 829

The original Coronation Pants were rather a clever idea first employed by King Egbert of Wessex. In AD 829 Egbert had managed to take over Kent, Essex, Sussex and Surrey and eventually he found himself controlling most of the area known as Mercia, which went as far north as a tiny mud village called Buminnam. Because he had done so well people began to refer to him as the First King of All England. This was a bit of a lie, as there were actually several areas that he wasn't in charge of at all, so the First King of Quite a Lot of England might have been a better title.

As there hadn't been a King of Quite-a-Lot-of-England before, they didn't have a proper ready-made crown for him, so he quickly fashioned a crown out of mud with a few bits of straw sticking

out of it. The trouble was
that a lot of other people
copied it and pretended to
be the king too, so to prove
that he was the real king,
Egbert fitted himself up with a
pair of special royal pants.

THE ORIGINAL
CROWN
JEWELS

These pants were made from
the strongest, thickest horsehair string and were
embroidered with gold thread by a nun in
Winchester, which at that time was England's capital
city. Egbert wore these pants all the time, so if ever
he got into an argument with a stranger about who
was king, he could prove his status by lowering his
leggings and revealing the royal pants. Little did
Egbert realize then that he had started a tradition
that would last until the present day. Egbert's
pants were destined to be on a royal posterior
for posterity.

Over the next 40 years these unique pants were
handed down from king to king. As they still didn't
have a proper crown, they just used a helmet with
"king" written on it. However, they found that this
was not ideal, as anyone could creep up behind the
king, snatch the helmet from his head and then run
off to wreak havoc pretending that they were the
rightful monarch. The pants were much harder to

pinch than the crown, so it was soon accepted that the helmet was nothing more than a sign to indicate who the king might be, and that the real proof lay in the royal pants.

When Egbert died he was succeeded by his son Ethelwulf, and then by Egbert's three grandsons Ethelbald, Ethelbert and Ethelred. Fortunately they were all roughly the same size so the pants did not need to be altered.

THE GUSSET EXTENSION, AD 871–944

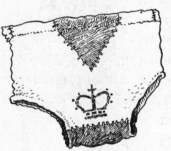

It was when Egbert's fourth grandson became king that the problems started. Alfred the Great succeeded the throne in AD 871, but the coronation ceremony was a bit awkward. Although the king's helmet fitted on his head quite well, Alfred was too great to pull the pants on. People could only stand and watch while Alfred hung around with no pants on, waiting until an emergency nun arrived to save the day.

It wasn't until she had spliced in a new section of waistband and a gusset extension that Alfred could pull the pants on and get on with the business of running the country. After Alfred died in 899, his son

Edward the Elder stepped into the royal pants, and then in 925 Edward's son Aethelstan pulled them on.

Aethelstan found that the royal pants were a bit baggy, but instead of having them altered he concentrated on taking over the far north of the country, including the particularly difficult area of Northumbria. By the time he died and passed the crown and pants on to his half-brother Edmund in 939, he was King of All England.

At first Edmund was so proud to be wearing Alfred's great pants that he had them painted purple with nice yellow stars – and thus he became known as "Edmund the Magnificent". But before long the new king found that the huge royal pants flapping about under his clothes were so distracting that he accidentally allowed Northumbria to be invaded by Olaf Guthfrithson. It wasn't until 944 that he had the gusset extension removed and the waistband tightened, and was thus able to concentrate on kicking Olaf out again.

DECAY AND DISPLAY 975

In AD 946 Edmund's little brother Eadred became the tenth king to step into the royal pants, which were now over 120 years old. It was no wonder that they were starting to show signs of wear and tear, and the fact that they were next worn by Eadred's two teenage sons in succession didn't help. Eadwig wore them until 959 and then his younger brother Edgar seized them. By the time Edgar died in 975, there was very little left of the original horsehair string, and the gold thread was almost worn away to nothing. The decayed royal pants could have been mistaken for any old pants, and this nearly lead to a very serious constitutional problem.

COULD YOU TELL WHICH PAIR WERE THE REAL ROYAL PANTS?

When Edgar died the pants passed on to his older son, Edward the Martyr. At the time they were still using a helmet with "king" marked on it for a crown, and Edward was only 12 when he first put it on.

Sadly for him, a lot of people would have preferred Edward's even younger half-brother Ethelred to be king and it wasn't long before the seven-year-old Ethelred also had a little helmet with "king" written on it. To settle the dispute Edward assembled all the barons and bishops, and in the time-honoured way he lowered his leggings to show that he was wearing the royal pants. There was a shocked silence when everyone just saw a few old horse hairs stuck around Edward's lower regions. Surely these could not be the pants of the king? At that moment everyone was all set to recognize Ethelred as the king, until Edward challenged Ethelred to lower his leggings and show a better pair of royal pants. Everyone turned to Ethelred expectantly. If Ethelred had been wearing any pants at all he would have been declared the true monarch, but unfortunately the little boy had made a silly mistake – he had forgotten to put on any pants that morning. All he could do was stutter and mumble excuses that the royal pants were in the wash, but it was clear that he was lying, and so they told him to take off his helmet, and on no account was he to do any reigning.

In the end it didn't do King Edward much good. Three years later he was visiting his half-brother and was assassinated, probably by Ethelred's mother. Edward's remains were put in a tomb at Shaftsbury and because they caused miracles to happen, he was made a saint. Sadly, one miracle that did not happen was any improvement to the royal pants. If anything, they got worse.

PANTS CUT DOWN, AD 978

King Ethelred II was only 10 when he first wore the pants in AD 978, so he had large sections cut from the waistband, gusset and both twangs to make them fit. He was known as Ethelred the Unready because he was never ready for anything, in particular the Vikings' surprise invasions. In the end he had to bribe them to go away. Another thing he wasn't ready for was growing too big for his pants, and by the time he died aged 38, the pants he'd had altered to fit him as a boy had grown very, very tight.

STRETCH
CREEAAK
STRAIN

That's how his son King Edmund II got a curious nickname. At his coronation in 1016 it took several nobles to pull the royal pants right up for Edmund, but they were so impressed that he didn't scream out in pain as the twangs scraped all the skin off his thighs, they called him Edmund Ironside.

Edmund was only king for a few months, and for most of this time he was battling with Canute from Denmark. In the end they reached an agreement by which Canute could be King of All England Apart From Wessex, but when Edmund dropped dead a few weeks later, Canute became King of All England Including Wessex. Canute probably thought this was good news until he realized that he had to pull on a very small pair of utterly disgusting ragged horsehair pants.

KING CANUTE AND THE SCANDANAVIAN INSERTS, 1016–42

King Canute knew that he had to do something about the pants, but he couldn't just take them off to be altered. As he was the first English king to have gained the royal pants by fighting rather than by inheritance, he didn't want to risk being caught with his pants down for even a few seconds. Therefore he concocted a plan so fantastic that even today some historians don't believe it really happened.

To start with, in 1019 he managed to become King of Denmark, and later, in 1028, he also became King of Norway. Of course this gave him lots of extra power and money and soldiers to order around, but the most important thing to Canute was that he managed to get his hands on the Danish and Norwegian royal pants.

It was around this time that some of his devoted followers started claiming that the King was so powerful he could even control the sea. Canute cleverly decided to prove how silly this rumour was, and at the same time gain the opportunity of having the pants altered. The well-known story tells of how Canute had his throne placed on a beach at low tide, then as the water came in he commanded the waves not to wet him. Of course the sea came in and everybody ran for it apart from Canute, who just stayed sitting where he was and getting soaked.

The story of Canute and the waves had always seemed a bit far-fetched until pantologists discovered the real reason for this bizarre event. Just as the sea was coming in and everybody was too busy running away to notice, Canute took the chance to slip off the old royal pants and pass them to an emergency nun. He knew that while he was sitting with the sea all around him, nobody was going to come up and pinch his king helmet or look at his pants, so he was safe. Meanwhile the emergency nun hurried away and very cleverly stitched the Danish and Norwegian royal pants into the old royal pants to make one nice big comfortable pair of royal pants.

When the tide went out again, she was the first to hurry back and pass over the revamped pants so he could put them on and continue reigning until 1035. Thereafter his sons Harold Harefoot and then Hardicanute wore the pants until 1042.

THE ROYAL PANTS TAKE A BACK SEAT

The pants maintained their importance for over 200 years because in all this time there had never really been a proper crown. It wasn't until the coronation of Edward the Confessor in 1042 that a shiny crown with gold bits appeared, and some of this gold is still part of the crown worn by Elizabeth II today. As the crown had suddenly become so much nicer, the pants started to lose their importance, but that didn't stop them making their mark on several occasions.

King Edward the Confessor was the son of Ethelred the Unready, and he also happened to have the same mother as the last king, Hardicanute. You might think that this would make everybody happy about him coming to the throne but they weren't.

Not even his mother liked him, so Edward spent most of his time hiding in church, confessing things. In particular the royal pants had got rather whiffy and when people wondered where the smell was coming from he kept confessing: "It's me. Sorry, yes, it's me again. Yes, I confess, it's still me..."

While he was busy confessing he let other people do the fighting and running the country for him, especially Godwine, Earl of Wessex. Edward had lived a lot of his life in France, and he had promised that when he died his cousin William of Normandy could be the next king, but on his deathbed in January 1066, Godwine's son Harold just happened to be passing and managed to grab the nice crown. As an afterthought he also took the royal pants – but the pants were to be Harold's undoing.

A SEVERED WAISTBAND AND THE BATTLE OF HASTINGS, 1066

Lots of people were unhappy about Harold being king, including his own brother Tostig, who borrowed the Norwegian army and invaded England. In 1066 Harold had to take his army north and managed to defeat Tostig at the battle of Stamford Bridge, but during the battle the waistband of the royal pants became severed.

Almost immediately Harold heard that William was invading in the south, so within three weeks he had dragged his exhausted army all the way to the other end of the country for the Battle of Hastings.

Unfortunately this didn't give him any time to contact an emergency nun to get the pants fixed. During the battle he found himself on top of a hill, giving orders and protecting himself by holding his shield over his head. But suddenly he felt his pants falling down. As he reached to pull them back up, he lowered his shield – and that's when an arrow hit him in the eye and killed him.

THE FIRST ITEM IN THE DOMESDAY BOOK, 1086

King William I, or William the Conqueror, as he became known, was horrified at the state of the royal pants and immediately summoned a team of emergency nuns to wash them. However, the nuns complained that it wasn't worth their time heating up water and getting the soap out just for one pair of pants, so they suggested that he made a list of anything else he needed doing. William first drew up a list of all his clothes, and then went on to list everything he had. He was so proud of it that he decided to make a list of everybody he knew and everything that they owned, and before long he had ordered a complete list of absolutely everybody and everything in the country. The final list was put into a massive book called the Domesday Book, which was then passed to the nuns. Not surprisingly the nuns rather wished they'd kept their mouths shut in the first place, so they discretely gave the pants a quick wash, handed them back and crossed them off the list. (That's why the royal pants do not appear in the Domesday Book.)

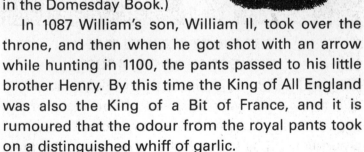

GLEAM

SHINE

In 1087 William's son, William II, took over the throne, and then when he got shot with an arrow while hunting in 1100, the pants passed to his little brother Henry. By this time the King of All England was also the King of a Bit of France, and it is rumoured that the odour from the royal pants took on a distinguished whiff of garlic.

Henry I died in 1135, and his daughter Matilda immediately decided it was her turn to be queen. However, Matilda didn't have many friends, especially when she took a sniff of the 300-year-old garlicky royal pants and announced it was time for a new pair. This insult caused all the nobles in the land to seize the pants and hand them over to Henry's nephew Stephen instead. King Stephen was a nice chap, and made up for Matilda's disappointment by letting her son Henry Plantagenet be the next king.

THE PLANTAGENETS

By this time everybody was used to identifying the king by his crown, and so there was less and less documentation regarding the royal pants. Pantologists are particularly frustrated that there is no proof that King Henry II (1154–89) was really known as Henry Pant-agenet, but it was some consolation to them when they discovered an item of pantological interest concerning the murder of his friend Thomas Becket. Henry had made Thomas the Archbishop of Canterbury, but when Thomas started taking the job too seriously, Henry joked that his pants were a lot holier than the Archbishop.

Thomas Becket refused to laugh, even when Henry explained it was a really good joke about having holes in his pants. Henry ended up losing his temper and uttered the unfortunate words, *"Who will rid me of this turbulent priest?"* Immediately four knights hurried off to murder Thomas Becket at the altar of Canterbury Cathedral.

THE ACT OF PANTS, 1170

Henry was so upset about the death of Thomas Becket that in 1170 he passed the Private Act of Pants, which decreed that the royal pants should become a state secret. Since then there has been no official acknowledgement that King Egbert's original pants have remained in use, but happily there is evidence to indicate that they have continued to be passed from monarch to monarch since that time as you'll see later on.

THE EPIC BALLAD OF SIR PANTSALOT

Back in those days there were no newspapers or radio or television, so one of the main ways to spread a story was by turning it into a song or a poem. Accounts of fierce battles, tales of bravery and victorious heroes could all be written in verse and then performed by touring minstrels for anyone who was interested. Of course, just like the news today, most of these stories would eventually go out of date and be forgotten, but fortunately a few have survived. Pantologists discovered this one carved on the wall of the parish church of Little Doings-in the-Fields.

ack in the autumn of 1257
when chivalry was at its height,
if you didn't like farming or going to church,
the best job was to be a knight.

Great stories are told about many such men,
for instance Sir Vanity Flash,
who carried two swords: one to slay dragons,
the other to trim his moustache.

Sir Whiffy the Pong wore his armour so long
the smell took the skin off a pig,
and Sir Baldy the Hairless's brain cooked to death
when lightning set fire to his wig.

Sir Starkers the Undressed was specially liked
although he was a bit silly.
On cold winter mornings he'd ride without clothes
and everyone saw he was chilly.

But this tale concerns one particular knight,
so handsome the ladies did weep.
They would tremble and sigh if he ever rode by
and they'd mutter his name in their sleep.

"Sir Pantsalot" (which is what he was called)
was noble and kind and sincere;
his manners were perfect, he dressed to impress
and he took a bath twice every year.

The other knights really despised how the ladies
attacked him like fleas on a dog.
It left them with minimal hope of a kiss
and no chance of a ten-minute snog.

Now it so came to pass that one bright day in June
a tournament battle was planned,
to be held on the banks of the great river Ouse
for every knight in the land.

The rules were quite simple, cruel but fair,
together the knights would arrive
and wallop each other with lances and swords,
until just the last did survive.

The winner would then be officially handed
a chalice of gold with a lid
covered in glittering diamonds and pearls,
and worth nearly forty-five quid.

Now forty-five quid was a lot in those days,
t'was enough for a knight to retire,
so instead of just rescuing damsels from dragons
he'd sit knitting socks by his fire.

A trumpeter trumped to announce the proceedings
were presently due to commence,
so the knights all got mounted which caused all the
ladies to wolf-whistle over the fence.

Now, back in those days they had a quaint custom
that before any fight could begin,
the ladies would offer a token of luck
to the knight that they wanted to win.

The token, an item of clothing,
was carefully chosen because
the feelings the lady might have for the knight
could be judged by
what her token was.

A glove would just indicate friendship,
a scarf might suggest a romance,
but a steaming-hot passionate promise of love
was shown by a nice pair of pants.

So when all the ladies saw handsome Sir Pantsalot,
and heard his great masculine laugh,
they knew what they wanted to give him at once,
and it wasn't a glove or a scarf.

As each of the knights were announced to the crowd
the ladies gave muted applause,
but on hearing "Sir Pantsalot" they dashed to the
bushes and hurriedly whipped off their drawers.

"Take mine," cried the first, "And mine," cried another,
"And MINE," cried out every girl there.
And soon good Sir Pantsalot was totally interred
in a mountain of warm underwear.

Among the grand duchesses, ladies and dames,
there was one pretty maiden named Lotte,
and unlike the others, whose pants were all plain,
her pants were bright red and spotty.

But in the confusion of ladies and lingerie
Lotte had got left behind,
so when the time came to pass over her pants
the knight just politely declined.

But Lotte was not to take no for an answer,
and just before off he did ride,
she jumped on his horse, ripped open his helmet
and shovelled her knickers inside.

The visor came down, she leapt to the ground
and slapped the knight's horse on the bot.
"Good luck," she did cry with a tear in her eye,
and into the battle he shot.

But Pantsalot needed a lot more than luck,
as he thrashed about blindly because
Lotte had covered his face with her pants
and he hadn't a clue where he was.

The other knights all had been fighting for ages
but suddenly came to a stop –
for when this great mountain of pants
rode towards them,
all their jaws open did drop.

Sir Whiffy, Sir Baldy, Sir Vanity Flash
were so jealous they started to sob.
For between them they'd just had one glove that they'd
used to cover Sir Starkers's gob.

Together they turned on Sir Pantsalot and
the look on their faces was grim –
they'd given up caring who might win the chalice
as long as it couldn't be him.

Down from his horse they did smash him, then pulled
their swords out to finish him quick,
but on lifting his visor they saw the red spots
and they all felt immediately sick.

"The plague!" they all cried. "He's got the plague!"
and all of their kneecaps did quiver.
And then to a man they all turned and ran,
and threw themselves into the river.

"What a result!" Sir Pantsalot cried
as he pulled Lotte's pants from his eyes.
"The others have legged it and therefore I've won,
so don't mess about, gimme the prize."

"I think you owe it to this little maiden,"
the prize-giving official said.
"If it wasn't for Lotte and her pants so spotty,
by now you'd be guaranteed dead."

"So what do you want of me?" Pantsalot asked.
"Whatever you ask for I'll give."
"Your hand in marriage I'll take," she did say.
"And happy e'er after we'll live."

"Then call for the parson at once," cried the knight,
"for I know I'll be happy with Lotte.
One glance at her pants told me all that I needed
for my pants, they also are spotty."

The parson then asked, "Do you both take each other?"
and they both replied that they did.
And so they became man and wife with a chalice
worth nearly forty-five quid.

The moral of this tale is simple to tell:
the might of the sword and the lance
is nothing compared to the true love declared
by a nice pair of red spotty pants.

The Pant Tax

Back in the thirteenth century, pant material was heavily taxed to raise money for the Crusades, and so the serfs had to make their pants from anything they could find. But how do we know about these pants? Fortunately, the remains of a pair of pants like this were found wrapped around a skeleton discovered in a Norfolk bog. Immediately a leading team of pantologists made a careful examination of the bones and discovered that these pants had been so troublesome that the peasant had caused his own death by completely scratching the whole of his bottom away.

Not surprisingly, even the poorest peasants soon realized that the only suitable material for making pants was pant material – but what could they do to make sure they paid as little tax as possible? This pair of pants shows one ingenious solution:

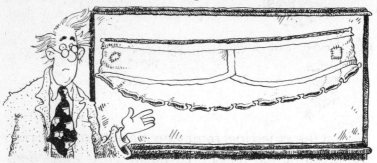

Several families could all wear this pair of pants at the same time, thus sharing the amount of tax that needed to be paid. But although these pants would have proved very cosy in winter, they did have one obvious disadvantage: nobody could pull their trousers right up to the top. The peasants had to think of something else pretty quickly if they wanted to avoid paying too much Pant Tax, and when they hit upon the answer, it turned out to be a landmark in the development of pantology. The answer was, of course ... the thong.

The thong evolved from the process of taking the original pant design, and seeing how much could be trimmed away. At first the results were not a success – as these examples excavated from the site of an old pantmakers shop demonstrate.

① ORIGINAL PANTS

② REMOVE SIDE TWANGS

③ REMOVE ONE SIDE

④ REMOVE ALL BUT WAISTBAND

First they tried just removing the side twangs, but the unsupported gusset fell down. Next they tried completely removing one side entirely, but this not only proved uncomfortable, but also the wearer tended to walk round in circles. A more radical step was to remove everything but the waistband. These pants stayed up perfectly, but sadly did not give the full levels of comfort and support that a pant-wearer might hope for.

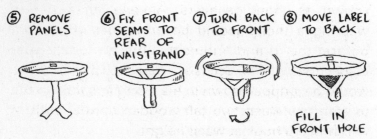

⑤ REMOVE PANELS

⑥ FIX FRONT SEAMS TO REAR OF WAISTBAND

⑦ TURN BACK TO FRONT

⑧ MOVE LABEL TO BACK

FILL IN FRONT HOLE

Next they tried removing all the panels while leaving the dangling seams intact. Although the results were regarded as highly fashionable in certain parts of Europe, the breakthrough really came when the front seams were brought back and attached to the rear of the waistband. Suddenly people had a completely revolutionary idea – they turned their pants front to back. The label was moved round, the small triangular hole was filled in with the minimum amount of pant material and the thong was born!

The Pantish Inquisition

From its earliest days the thong caused outrage, especially as some people kept their Pant Tax to a minimum by not filling in the front panel. By the fifteenth century, many religious leaders in Spain were so concerned at the unrespectable state of people's underwear, they sought out the heretics known as thong-believers. Anyone suspected of wearing a thong would be arrested and brought before the grand inquisitor for an underwear inspection. If the accused was found guilty, he would be stripped down to his thong and then made to stand between two tall wooden stakes, each of which had a hook at waist height.

The sides of the thong were then pulled outwards away from the body and slipped over the hooks. Two large hooded monks would then grab the prisoner and turn him head over heels round and round and round, winding up the sides of the thong as tight as they would go. Finally they would stand well back, just holding on to the prisoner's feet. On a signal from the inquisitor they would let go. The prisoner would spin round at terrifying speed as the thong unwound; usually the prisoner would spin so fast that his arms and legs flew out of their sockets.

The Ice Pants

This water is taken from a puddle discovered on the floor of a ruined monastery in Bavaria. Pantologists believe that this may be the remains of a pair of ice pants, worn by fifteenth-century German monks as a punishment for having a dirty habit.

RESTORATION PANTS
The Royal Pants in the Sixteenth and Seventeenth Centuries

Pantologists sniffing around for clues regarding the progress of the pants picked up the scent while studying the death of King Edward VI. His father Henry VIII reigned between 1509 and 1547. Now, Henry was a big man who enjoyed a lot of tennis, fighting, wives, organ-playing and other sorts of exercise, so after 38 years the state of the royal pants can only be imagined. What's more, he spent his final months being extremely diseased in bed, so when the pants were finally peeled off his dead body, the next wearer would need to have been very robust to survive them. Sadly his son and heir, Edward, was a feeble child, and when he became king at the age of ten the smell of the pants was enough to flatten a carthorse. No wonder the young King Edward VI was sick for five years and then finally gave up and died in 1553. Edward is the only English monarch who is suspected to have died of acute pantosis.

The royal pants then passed to Mary, the first ever Queen of England (Matilda didn't really count). She is known to have burnt hundreds of people at the stake for being Protestant – but what could have put her in such a foul mood? To pantologists the answer is obvious. Mary was required to wear a pair of pants that had already been worn by over 40 men, as far as anyone knew they had only ever been washed once, by William I, and both her father and her half-brother had died in them. No wonder she was a bit tetchy.

Mary didn't have to wear the pants for long – they finally overpowered her in 1558, and passed to her half-sister, Elizabeth I, who wore them for 45 years. This may explain why she never married. By the time she died in 1603 they were in serious need of repair. Thankfully the next monarch of England was King James I (who was also King James VI of Scotland). He had the royal pants patched up with bits from the Scottish royal pants, and he also had the biggest holes carefully sewn over with strong wool. The process of filling in pant holes is known as "darning" and was named after James's father Lord Darnley.

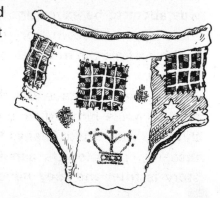

HOW FAMOUS PEOPLE DRIED THEIR PANTS
NO. 3 GUY FAWKES

Condemned Pants, 1649

When King James died in 1625 his son Charles took over, and it is thanks to him that pantologists have some evidence as to the condition of the royal pants. On the morning of 30 January 1649 Charles was about to be executed. It was a chilly day, and there is a well-known story that before heading out to the scaffold the monarch asked for a second shirt to wear.

The reason he gave was that he did not wish the cold to make him shiver and so have the people think he was afraid. Thanks to years of painstaking research, pantologists can now confirm that this story is true, and they have even discovered one further detail. Just to make absolutely sure there were no other signs that he might be afraid, the King also put on a second pair of pants. Presumably the original royal pants were in such a state of decay, their discretion at a time of crisis could not be relied upon. The Act of Pants had decreed that mention of the royal pants was punishable by death, but as Charles was being executed anyway, nobody made a fuss.

The Pirates of Pants

Around the year 1700, the seas around the West Indies were plagued by ruthless pirates, renowned for their cruelty and barbarism. Among the worst offenders was a pirate named Blackpants, so called because he had never in his life changed his underwear. When sailors saw the distinctive flag on Blackpants' ship *The Grimy Cleft* approaching, they would immediately try to race away, but it was usually in vain. Once Blackpants had drawn up alongside his victim's ship, those that knew of him would throw themselves into the sea and take their chances with the sharks rather than suffer at his hands. For those that did not manage to get away, a truly sickening ordeal was in store.

The captives would be herded down a trapdoor into the smallest, darkest hold of their boat. Standing on the deck above them, Blackpants would remove his black pants. He would dangle the dripping, mouldy undies over their heads for a moment to let his victims see the green vapours that were oozing from the leg holes, and then with an evil cackle he would drop his pants down and slam the trapdoor shut. As the screams, choking and retching started in the hideous darkness, Blackpants would dance a jig on the trapdoor and sing the following shanty:

I stole my pants in Bristol,
from a tramp laid in the gutter.
I shot him with my pistol,
then I sailed off to Calcutta.

Oh...
... my pants have been a-sailing here,
and there and everywhere.
Jammed right up my bottom,
where there is no fresh air.

Then I sailed to Botany Bay
and the Cape of Good Hope,
and never once along the way
have they seen any soap.

He would then call through the trapdoor, offering a reward to anyone who could join him in the chorus, but of course it was just a cruel joke. If one or two brave souls hoped to gain their freedom by singing *"Oh my pants have been a-sailing here..."* he would open the trapdoor, drop in one of his socks, then slam it shut again.

HOW FAMOUS PEOPLE DRIED THEIR PANTS

NO. 4 ADMIRAL NELSON

ENGLAND EXPECTS EVERY MAN TO WEAR CLEAN PANTS...

Hanging by Twangs

Although 500 years had passed since the original Pant Tax was introduced, it had never been properly repealed. As a consequence, a fine pair of pants was still a luxury reserved for the rich, and so it was no wonder they attracted the attentions of criminals.

In the year 1739, one of the country's most notorious highwaymen was executed in Knavesmire Woods. Of course there were many other highwaymen robbing travellers in those days, but

99

what made this one exceptional was that instead of stealing money and jewels, he used to steal the pants of the rich. On many occasions a coachful of anxious travellers would suddenly find themselves staring down the barrel of a musket and hearing those fateful words:

STAND AND DELIVER – YOUR UNDIES OR YOUR LIFE!!

This evil highwayman was a man named Dick Burpin. When he was finally caught and arrested the authorities decided to make an example of him. They planned his execution so that the punishment fitted the crime.

Dick Burpin's hoard of underwear was seized and from it was selected the largest and strongest pair of pants. Burpin had his hands bound and was taken to stand underneath the overhanging branch of a large oak tree. One leg hole of the pants was hooked on to the branch, then three stout yeomen stretched the other leg hole right down and forced the felon's head through it. When they released the pants, the elastic pulled Dick Burpin clear of the ground. There he swung until he died, hung by his own twangs.

The French Revolution, 1789

Some 50 years later, the Pant Tax was also the cause of rebellion across the channel in France. The French aristocracy were very rich, while the peasants were very poor – and this unhappy situation led to the French Revolution. Not only did the rich have fantastic houses and food and servants, they also showed their contempt for the Pant Tax by wearing huge heavily embroidered pants. In contrast, the peasants lived in poverty with little or no food, and thanks to the Pant Tax, they had no chance of affording even the skimpiest pants.

One of the most hated figures in France at the time was Marie Antoinette, the wife of King Louis XVI. She used to boast that the tax on her pants would be enough to feed a small town. Curiously she was also known for having a very tiny waist, as shown by this selection from her pant wardrobe:

BREAKFAST PANTS

RIDING PANTS

WALTZING PANTS

Marie Antoinette is famous for making two remarks that especially upset the peasants. On hearing about the starving families that had no bread to eat she famously said: "Let them eat cake." This callous remark caused a lot of deep resentment, but worse was to come. When Marie Antoinette heard that the peasants had no pants to wear, she blurted out: "Let them wear boxer shorts." It was at that moment that the Revolution started.

The peasants rose up and attacked the nobles, many of whom (including Marie Antoinette) had their heads chopped off at the guillotine. But some of the nobles were saved by a mysterious figure known as "the Scarlet Panternel". He was an English aristocrat who diguised himself by pulling a scarlet pair of pants over his head and peering out of the leg holes. If ever he was being chased by the peasants, all he had to do was whisk his pants off and blend into the crowd. The only tell-tale signs were certain lingering odours around his face, and hence the popular ditty of the time:

They sniff him here, they sniff him there,
Those Frenchies sniff him everywhere.
Is he in heaven or is he in hell
That damned malodorous Panternel!

Mutiny on the Wedgie

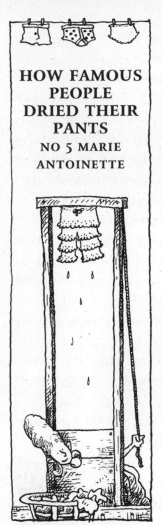

HOW FAMOUS PEOPLE DRIED THEIR PANTS
NO 5 MARIE ANTOINETTE

At the same time as the French Revolution, another notorious pants incident was happening on the other side of the world. In 1789 the grand sailing ship HMS *Wedgie* was heading across the South Pacific Ocean carrying a precious cargo of new pants, under the command of the brutal Captain Tights. It had been a long and difficult voyage, with temperatures and tempers both running hot, food and water both running out, and the sailors own pants in desperate need of a wash. One or two of them had brought a spare pair, but these had been traded or gambled away at cards, and the whole ship was facing a pants crisis. Nevertheless, Captain Tights refused to let them help themselves to any of the cargo and this led to the sailors plotting a mutiny. One night, when the officers were all asleep, they seized control of the boat. Anyone who resisted was thrown overboard to the sharks, but for the evil captain himself they prepared a different fate.

First they undressed him down to his pants, then they tied his feet to the deck of the ship with a thick rope. Next they took two very long ropes and tied one to each of the side twangs of the captain's pants. They threw the other ends of the ropes high up over the yardarms, then pulled down the two loose ends. Several strong men took hold of each rope and started to heave. The ropes tightened and started to hoist the captain's pants higher and higher up his body.

Soon the side twangs had stretched up past his shoulders, causing the gusset to dig in tighter and tighter. As the captain's agonized screams echoed across the water, the men heaved on until both side twangs were touching the yardarm high above the deck. Just as it seemed that the captain would be split in two from the bottom upwards by the tension in his pants, the first mate took a knife and cut through the rope tying his feet to the deck.

The captain was fired upwards as though from a catapult. He shot several miles up into the sky and was never seen again.

This dreadful act has since been recreated many times to a lesser degree, and even today is still known as a "Wedgie", after the ship on which it first occurred.

HOW FAMOUS PEOPLE DRIED THEIR PANTS
NO. 6 COUNT PANTULA OF PANTZYLVANIA

The Age of Invention

The nineteenth and twentieth centuries saw advances in many forms of technology, including engineering, textiles, transport and of course, pants. Many pantologists devoted long hours to taking the humble pant and adapting it to perfom all sorts of interesting functions. Here are just a few...

George Stephenson's Pantomotive

George Stephenson built his steam-powered pantomotive in 1820. The initial tests were made on a track near Darlington, and a curious crowd had gathered to watch. The tester and driver, a Mr Plumb, was wearing the pants and beside him Mr Willis the fireman was loading coal into the boiler. Once enough steam had built up, a man ran in front waving a red flag and Mr Plumb set off. Unfortunately, the pressure in the pants was too high and the boiler sprung a leak, causing steam to shoot out of the back and blow most of the crowd over.

Not all was lost, though, for within a few years Stephenson had adapted the pants into a railway engine, which ran along the Stockton-Darlington line. Of course, the fact that the first train was originally made from pants explains why even today the insides of many railway trains smell the way they do. Indeed, many people claim that the railways are still pants today.

HOW FAMOUS PEOPLE DRIED THEIR PANTS
NO. 7 GEORGE STEPHENSON

Brunel's Suspension Pants

One of the most exciting engineering achievements in the middle of the nineteenth century was the Clifton Suspension Bridge in Bristol. It was designed by the great engineer Isambard Kingdom Brunel, but until recently nobody knew where he got the idea. However, pantologists can now reveal that he was inspired one Monday morning after washing his pants.

Once they had been in the hot tub, he sprayed on some starch and then put them through the mangle, which squeezed them out into a much wider shape. As he took them to the washing line, he was thinking about bridges and not paying much attention to his pants, and so he accidentally hung them upside down...

... and design history was made.

The Cuckoo Clock Pants

Meanwhile in Switzerland, the cuckoo clock pants made a dramatic entrance. They were first worn by the president at a grand exhibition of Swiss technology set up to show the world how Switzerland was moving with the times. Unfortunately the president happened to start making his speech at one minute to twelve and was almost immediately drowned out when the cuckoo popped out to chime the hour. In his surprise the president fell over backwards and got his clock weights tangled up with his pendulum.

Dr Keckyll's Pantsuds

In the pioneering days of pantology, much research was made into the best method of cleaning pants. The results are taken for granted these days, but back then it was a very different story. What follows are entries from the laboratory notes of Dr Keckyll, written in the year 1888.

8 May 7:14 pm

At last! I think I have perfected my new "Pantsuds", a washing agent in the form of green salts. I have prepared a tub of warm water on the workbench and to it I have added a cupful of the agent. I note a pleasing layer of bubbles now covers the surface and the smell is fragrant. The time has come to add the pants which I wish to clean. I have chosen a sturdy pair of Sunday pants, respectable in every way and most suitable to be photographed should the results prove successful.

7:21 pm

The pants have been submerged for some minutes now, and so far no ill effects have been observed. I shall take my wooden laundry tongs and pull them out...

8:41 pm

What has happened? I wake on the floor of my laboratory, the bubbled water has splashed all around me and gone cold. A pane of the laboratory window is smashed, and of the Sunday pants there is no sign. I can only pray that they are safe.

9 May 10:32 am

A police constable has called to bring my pants home, having identified them by the laundry mark. They were found on the stage of the Royal Opera House after the theatre had been abandoned. Florence the housekeeper showed me the most extraordinary newspaper cutting:

THE PANT-OM OF THE OPERA

Last night's gala performance of La Petite Twee Naffette at the Royal Opera House was thrown into chaos during the highlight of the third half. Just as the enchanting love duet "Your Lips are Sweet as Cherry Blossom" was starting, a large hairy pair of pants burst on to the stage in a cloud of smoke and a crack of thunder, and proceeded to make some music of its own...

It seems the large hairy pants got away. How my Sunday pants came to be discovered there is a mystery. And yet as I notice the traces of make-up and stage oil on the gusset, I have a wild suspicion about what may have occurred. It is too fantastic to be credible, but just in case I think I'll check my Pantsuds formula.

13:14

Great heavens — I have found a most dangerous error in my calculations for the formula! The Pantsuds were designed to remove all the bad, nasty and unpleasant ingredients from a pair of pants, thus leaving only the good, wholesome, trustworthy components behind. But in arriving at the final formula, I accidentally placed a plus sign instead of a critical minus sign and thus the exact opposite result has been achieved! And this is why my well-behaved, docile Sunday pants have suddenly started acting in this abominable manner.

13:15

I am deeply ashamed of the behaviour of my pants.

13:16

How terrible that they should have jumped on to the stage at the Opera House.

13:17

But what fun it must have been, what excitement...

13:18

If only I was brave enough to do such things.

13:19

I wonder what the Pantsuds taste like...?

This is the last entry in Dr Keckyll's diary, but we do have a cutting from the next day's newspaper:

HORROR PANTS CAUSE WEDDING CAKE CARNAGE

It should have been the event of the year when the dashing Prince Freeload and his beautiful young bride Chavina Bling exchanged their tender vows in the cathedral. But less than three hours later it all ended in disaster. At the end of a sumptuous reception banquet, 200 doves were released to signify their love, but just as the couple were about to cut the magnificent wedding cake, a man wearing only a large hairy pair of pants jumped down from the ceiling, sat on the cake and squashed it to a mushy pulp.

The respected scientist Dr Keckyll is now helping police with their enquiries.

The Electric Pants

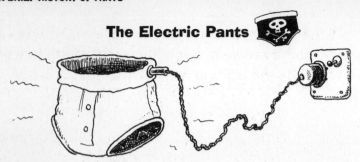

The first electrically heated pants were patented in America in 1909. On chilly winter mornings the "Cosy Cheeks" could be pulled on and then plugged into an electric socket to warm them up. Not surprisingly they caused an immediate sensation and caught the attention of the German nobleman Count Wedje. He ordered a pair without realizing that they were designed for use with the American 110-volt system. As soon as they arrived he tore them eagerly from the packet, put them on and plugged them into an electric socket by his bedside. Unfortunately for the count, European sockets deliver 220 volts, which came as a great shock to him...

Running Pants

The nitroglycerine rocket pants were used unsuccessfully by Malesh Dingbo in the 1946 Olympic 100-metre trials. The pants accelerated so fast that Malesh's feet crossed the winning line in under three seconds. Sadly the top half of Malesh was still on the starting line.

HOW FAMOUS PEOPLE DRIED THEIR PANTS
NO. 8 THE YETI
(OR THE ABOMINABLE SNOWMAN)

PANTS AT WAR

This section of the museum is devoted to those unsung and forgotten heroes of the war. They operated under cover in difficult and often inhospitable conditions, and so it is all too easy to forget the contribution made to the war effort by military pants. Many different types were developed for different purposes.

Communication Pants

If a secret agent wanted to send a secret message across a busy room to a contact, he might use his special communication pants, which would emit a burst of unintelligible noise. Although it sounded like a perfectly natural bodily function, the contact could use a pair of receiving pants to decode the noise into a message. To show that the message had been received and understood, the contact would then give a secret sign by asking for a window to be opened.

For long-distance messages, special carrier pants were used. These pants contained a selection of special marks that represented coded messages. The pants would make their way across Europe, hopping between laundry baskets and hitching rides on different wearers. Once the pants arrived at their destination, they would be opened up and the message decoded. In case the pants were intercepted, dummy pants were also used with false marks to throw the enemy off the scent.

Escape Pants

These old pants were designed to help people escape enemy prison camps.

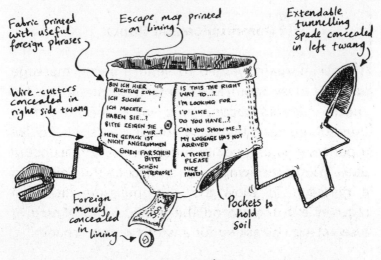

Fabric printed with useful foreign phrases

Escape map printed on lining

Extendable tunnelling spade concealed in left twang

Wire-cutters concealed in right side twang

BIN ICH HIER RICHTUG ZUM...?
ICH SUCHE...
ICH MOCHTE...
HABEN SIE...?
BITTE ZEIGEN SIE MIR...?
MEIN GEPACK IST NICHT ANGEKOMMEN
EINEN FARSCHEIN BITTE
SCHÖN UNTERHOSE!

IS THIS THE RIGHT WAY TO...?
I'M LOOKING FOR...
I'D LIKE...
DO YOU HAVE...?
CAN YOU SHOW ME...?
MY LUGGAGE HAS NOT ARRIVED
A TICKET PLEASE
NICE PANTS!

Foreign money concealed in lining

Pockets to hold soil

Gadget Pants

There were also special gadget pants fitted with a range of devices to help agents in the field.

More recently "stealth pants" have been invented, which enable the wearer to change his trousers completely undetected by the enemy (unless of course the enemy is wearing "heat-seeking" pants), and magnetic pants are used by aeroplane pilots to hold them in their seats when they fly upside down. Possibly the most famous of all military pants are Swiss Army pants, which come fitted with lots of useful tools, including a bottle-opener, a nail file, a thing for taking stones out of horses' hooves and a toilet-paper dispenser.

Personally I enjoy wearing my gyroscopic navigational pants, which always ensure that I'm pointing in the right direction.

PANTS TODAY
The Royal Pant Line – An Update

Sadly there are many fascinating things about the royal pants that will never be known.

• Did King John spill ink on them when he signed the Magna Carta in 1215?

• When King James VI of Scotland also became King James I of England, did he fit them with a sporran?

• Did William and Mary (joint monarchs until she died in 1694) wear the pants on alternate days? Or did they both wear them at the same time?

• Did mad King George III throw a millennium party for their 1,000th birthday in 1819? (If so then he really was mad because he would have been 10 years early.)

• When Queen Victoria first pulled the pants on, did she say "We are not amused"?

It is amazing to think of all the stories those pants could tell, but sadly the royal pants have always remained silent. Indeed, there has never been so much as a squeak out of them, and yet there are a few questions that could be answered. Do the pants still contain a few of Egbert's original horsehairs? Do they still have sections of the Danish and Norwegian pants sewn into them? Is it still possible to see where the waistband gave way at the Battle of Hastings? There is only one person in the whole world who could reveal all ... but she's sitting tight and refuses to let anything slip out.

The Exposure of Pants

Although the very first wearers of pants were proud to show them off, for many centuries pants were always worn discreetly under other items of clothing. It is only recently that modern fashion trends dictate that pants should again be on view. Having your pants on display not only assures others that you are wearing some, but it can also be of benefit in other ways.

Pants worn over tights always frighten criminals because they indicate that the wearer has super powers.

Here the displayed pants get big laughs, and so help the wearer make money.

This time the displayed pants detract an audience from terrible singing and ridiculous facial hair.

Although many people opt for rear thong exposure, pantologists are still investigating why anyone could possibly regard this as a good thing, unless it is to provide somewhere to carry a folded umbrella.

The Final Frontier

When pants were first invented, they only had to serve the two basic purposes of warmth and modesty. Nowadays so much more is required of the humble pant, especially when it comes to space missions.

When a rocket blasts off, the weight on board is kept to an absolute minimum, and therefore the astronauts have to do without many essentials that we take for granted, including a washing machine. Some space missions can last for up to six months, so if clean pants were to be worn every day, it would require about 180 pairs of pants to be packed for each astronaut. As this wouldn't leave much room for computers and telescopes a different scheme had to be devised, and this resulted in one of the most remarkable pieces of technology ever developed: the Self Washing Astronaut Pants, or "SWAPS".

SWAPS are made out of bendy plastic and are fitted with a microchip and a selection of wipers. During normal use the wipers are discreetly tucked into the waistband, but as soon as the sensors detect that the wearer is asleep, the cleaning cycle starts.

First a selection of tiny spray jets refresh the outside of the pants, then the wipers swing down and gently mop away any debris. Next comes the most remarkable part of the operation – the pants turn themselves inside out while still being worn. This is achieved by a selection of rollers around the waistband and leg holes that rotate all the various panels of the pants until the inside surfaces are on the outside and vice versa. Once again the jets and wipers come into operation and then the programme shuts down until the next cycle.

Fortunately, SWAPS rarely malfunction, but the most common problems occur when the wearer is sitting still for a long time, thus causing the cycle to unexpectedly switch on. This can take the wearer by surprise. (Interestingly, SWAPS are also in great demand on Earth by mothers who want to buy them for their teenage children.)

SWAPS can also be fitted with attachments:

• In case of space walks, a breathing tube can be attached to the pants.

• There is a tube for disposing of excess waste matter.

• There is a jet-powered nozzle at the back for flying around.

Naturally, one of the main parts of an astronaut's training is to ensure that these three devices are not connected the wrong way round.

**HOW FAMOUS PEOPLE
DRIED THEIR PANTS**
NO. 9 THE CREW OF THE APOLLO
SPACE MISSIONS

COULD YOU
BE A PANTOLOGIST?

PANTOLOGIST

I hope you've enjoyed your tour round my exhibits. By now you should have grasped the rudiments of pantology. But even though we've reached the end of the tour, for true pantologists history is only the beginning. The big question is where do we go from here? Pantologists believe that pants may be able to offer us the final answer.

Now that it has been established that so many events in history are pant-based, pantologists believe that time itself could be modelled on the Great Pant Cycle. Consider how pants are continually worn, washed and hung out to dry in never-ending repetition. Surely this is a clue to the future! All the signs indicate that the universe will come round full circle and in a few million years time the Pantasaurus will once again roam the Earth and the Homo Pantiens will pick up his second spear...

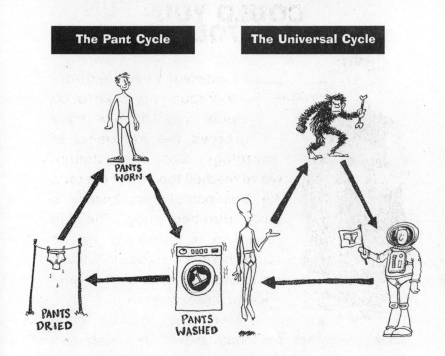

The Pant Cycle

PANTS WORN

PANTS DRIED

PANTS WASHED

The Universal Cycle

Of course this theory is far too complicated for normal people, but if you have read, understood and (most importantly of all) believed everything you've seen in **A Brief History of Pants**, then you are no longer normal. Not only will you understand the theory, but you can also proudly announce to the world that you are a fully qualified pantologist. Congratulations and welcome to the team!

WANT SOME MORE FUN WITH PANTS?

Amaze your friends and learn some pants tricks!